LOUDEN NELSON

FROM SLAVERY TO PHILANTHROPY

by Franklin Marshall
Illustrated by Maricela Marshall

PRINTERS Sentinel Printers, INC
SCANNING Bay Photo
DESIGN AND PRODUCTION Richard Curtis
Jacket photograph "Santa Cruz September 1st 1860"
courtesy of Sentinel Printers, INC

ISBN# 1-893931-01-3
Copyright © 2003
Published by Children's Learning Museum
PO Box 2598 Santa Cruz CA 95063
831-420-1765
www.childrenslearningmuseum.org
email clmuseum@cruzers.com

When Louden Nelson was a boy, he would wander dreaming of a land far away. There he could be like a bird, soaring into the beauty of nature, roaming free without a care in the world, growing his own garden, fishing, laughing, and occasionally singing a song. "How wonderful this would be", thought Louden.

But just as he was imagining a voice would call saying, "Louden, come down here and get some water." Louden was six years old and it was his mom calling him to do some chores around the house. Louden and his family were slaves in North Carolina. Louden didn't quite know what that meant.

He often played with his master's sons, Matthew, David, and William Nelson. They lived in the big white house out front. Louden and his family lived in the slave quarters with the other slaves. Louden grew and played, dreaming and having fun. Those days were fun but he didn't know that the more he grew, the less playtime he would have.

When Louden was ten years old,
there was a big change.

He no longer was allowed to spend time with
Matthew, David, and William, and would
only see them as he passed by on his way to
work in the field. Matthew, Master Nelson's
youngest son, often came over to him to
spend a little time talking.

One day Louden was talking
to his mother, while working
in the field he overheard
others talking about how
they dreamed of freedom and
not be slaves anymore.

Louden asked his mom,
"What is a slave?"

His mother said, "You are a slave when
someone else owns you and you don't have
freedom to do as you please. You must work
when they tell you to work. You eat when
they tell you. You eat what they tell you to
eat, they can even sell you to someone else if
they choose to."

This frightened Louden. Why did things have to be this way? Who can help us? Louden thought back to when he was six years old and dreaming about being free.

Now, in his young ten-year-old mind, he longed for freedom more than ever. Louden thought about freedom so much that he would often find himself in tears for his condition and the people around him.

Once he passed a church, he stopped to listen even though he was afraid of being caught. He heard someone praying, "Please God, please help." He decided that he would use the same words whenever he needed them – "Please God, help me."

Louden grew older. He worked hard. When he became a teenager he noticed that some of the people that worked on Master Nelson's Plantation were gone to some other farm. He knew they had been sold. He wondered, "Will this happen to me?"

Louden continued to work and tried to be
optimistic. When he was sad, he
remembered the dreams he had as a little
boy, of freedom, and this would bring
comfort to him.

As the years passed, Matthew grew to hate slavery, too. He thought, "Why can't people be free to think and do as they please?" He remembered how he and Louden had played together and the fun they had.

He still stopped to talk to
Louden when no one else was
nearby. He could never be
caught showing favoritism to
Louden. His father, Master
Nelson, would be very angry.

When Louden was still a young man in his thirties, Master Nelson became very ill and died. To Louden this was one of the most frightening times in his life. He worried about being sold to another plantation. He didn't know what would happen to him.

The Nelson brothers were given their father's estate to be divided among themselves. Matthew wanted his share to include Louden. He wanted to be able to offer him his freedom. Matthew negotiated for Louden and some other slaves to be given to him.

Matthew promised
Louden that if he
would come to
California to help him
dig for gold, he would
give him his freedom.
Louden could not
believe his ears,
freedom!

Matthew took his
money, Louden, and
several other slaves,
and headed first to
Tennessee and then
to California for a
new start.

Matthew worked hard alongside
the slaves he took with him to
California. Louden was there
to do whatever was needed as
Matthew dug and panned for
gold. Louden felt he was
getting closer and closer to his
freedom.

Within five years
Matthew had made his
fortune. He kept his
promise to Louden and
granted him his
freedom. Louden was no
longer a slave! Matthew
went back to his family
in Tennessee.

Louden was now a free man.
What to do?

Traveling from town to town, he searched
for a place to live where he could find his
childhood dream of living free. Finally, he
settled in Santa Cruz, a little town of only
800 people, where he was one of only two
freed slaves.

The people of Santa Cruz
liked Louden. He had a
pleasant manner that
characterized hospitality.

He got to know many of the town's people,

who frequently visited him at home.

Along with his freedom Matthew Nelson also gave Louden money, enough to allow him to buy land. Louden was a cobbler, a blacksmith, and a farmer and was handy at a number of other jobs. On his land he began a business of shoe making. He farmed the land and was successful in both businesses.

While in town one day, Louden heard that
the only school in Santa Cruz was closing.
The school was on the hill just above
Louden's home, where he could hear the
children playing every day.

Often when he was working, the children's voices took him back to when he was six years old, feeling free as a bird, enjoying the beauties of nature. Hearing the children laughing, singing, and playing were a pleasure for him. What would happen if the school closed down? Where would the children go to learn? This worried him and he wondered what he could do to help.

Louden continued to work hard
until he became sick and was unable
to work any longer. The people of
the town soon discovered Louden's
illness and helped care for him.

Louden's health got
worse. He knew he
was going to die.

During this time the school,
which Louden loved,
was on the brink
of closing.

There were no more funds to keep it open.
All Louden could think about was his
childhood dream of freedom and the beauty
of the children singing and laughing in the
school on the hill.

Louden vowed,
"As I was given freedom,
I will give my property
to keep this school open."

When Louden Nelson died, his property was left to the city of Santa Cruz. The school remained open, and as the years passed, the city grew; new schools were added. Today, the people of Santa Cruz are grateful to Louden for his generosity and for the help he gave to their first school. He gave a lifeline to Santa Cruz city's first school.